CHAPARRALS

Samantha Nugent

AV² provides enriched content that supplements and complements this book. Weigl's AV² books strive to create inspired learning and engage young minds in a total learning experience.

Your AV² Media Enhanced books come alive with...

Key Words
Study vocabulary, and complete a matching word activity.

Quizzes
Test your knowledge.

Slide Show
View images and captions, and prepare a presentation.

Audio
Listen to sections of the book read aloud.

Video
Watch informative video clips.

Embedded Weblinks
Gain additional information for research.

Try This!
Complete activities and hands-on experiments.

... and much, much more!

LET'S READ
AV² BY WEIGL™
ADDED VALUE • AUDIO VISUAL

Go to www.av2books.com, and enter this book's unique code.

BOOK CODE

K 3 8 7 2 3 2

AV² by Weigl brings you media enhanced books that support active learning.

Published by AV² by Weigl
350 5th Avenue, 59th Floor New York, NY 10118
Website: www.av2books.com

Library of Congress Control Number: 2015956109

ISBN 978-1-4896-4169-4 (hardcover)
ISBN 978-1-4896-4170-0 (softcover)
ISBN 978-1-4896-4171-7 (single-user eBook)
ISBN 978-1-4896-4172-4 (multi-user eBook)

Printed in the United States of America in Brainerd, Minnesota
1 2 3 4 5 6 7 8 9 0 19 18 17 16 15

122015
111315

Project Coordinator: Jared Siemens
Designer: Mandy Christiansen

The publisher acknowledges Corbis Images, Getty Images, Minden Pictures, Alamy, Shutterstock, and iStock as the primary image suppliers

CHAPARRALS

Contents

This is a chaparral.
A chaparral has many shrubs
and very hot summers.

4

Chaparrals are found near an ocean or large body of water. They are often found between deserts and grasslands.

The largest chaparral in the United States is in California.

Chaparrals are hot and dry for most of the year. Summer temperatures can be 115 degrees Fahrenheit (43 degrees Celsius).

Chaparral winters are mild and rainy.

Goats eat the leaves of poison oak trees.

Manzanita shrubs give shelter to birds and other small animals.

Costa's hummingbirds help new flowers grow.

Tammar wallabies get most of their water from plants.

A chaparral ecosystem is a place made up of animals and plants that need each other in order to live.

Trapdoor spiders eat insects that live on or near the ground.

Bumblebees eat
bee orchid nectar.

Cork oak trees
can live
through fires.

Trees, shrubs, and flowers
all grow in chaparrals.
They are an important part
of a chaparral ecosystem.

Cactus wrens live
in cholla cacti.

Coastal sage scrub leaves grow thicker in summer so they will not dry out.

Chamise is an important food for deer.

Gray foxes climb trees to look for food.

Horned lizards squirt blood out of their eyes to scare away predators.

Rattlesnakes use sharp fangs to catch food.

Many different animals make their homes in chaparrals.

Jackrabbits have large ears that help them stay cool.

California newts have poison in their skin so animals do not eat them.

15

Chaparrals get very little rain during summer. This is called a drought.

Chaparral plants get most of their water from fog during summer.

Some people live in chaparrals.
Dry leaves near their houses
can catch fire.

People can keep
their homes safe
by raking leaves
in their yards.

Large fires called wildfires take place in chaparrals. These fires can hurt people and animals. Dry plants make wildfires spread fast.

Firefighters start smaller fires to burn the dry plants. This helps keep people and animals safe from wildfires.

Chaparral Quiz

See what you have learned about chaparral ecosystems.

Find these chaparral animals and plants in the book. What are their names?

KEY WORDS

Research has shown that as much as 65 percent of all written material published in English is made up of 300 words. These 300 words cannot be taught using pictures or learned by sounding them out. They must be recognized by sight. This book contains 75 common sight words to help young readers improve their reading fluency and comprehension. This book also teaches young readers several important content words, such as proper nouns. These words are paired with pictures to aid in learning and improve understanding.